Introduction

Triangles are so versatile and are a standard unit in quilting. They come in many different sizes and angles. Many of the traditional patterns that use them have been around for years and years. Styles and fabrics change, but triangles remain an important element in quilts. The techniques for making them have also changed. Now there are rulers for easy, accurate cutting, or precise foundation piecing methods along with several traditional techniques. No matter how you make them, they are here to stay. The popularity of triangles tends to ebb and flow. Sometimes they're everywhere, and sometimes not so much. Today's quilter sees them everywhere.

No matter which way you decide to construct them, including triangle shapes in your quilts can add interest and beauty to them. *Trendy Triangles* is a collection of eight outstanding designs for today's quilter. These timeless patterns were selected for their unique style and variety—patterns that are in line with trends in the quilting community. Study them and use your imagination to see your own fabric choices in them.

Triangles are an important part of quilt designs and are much easier to construct than you might think. The options are endless, so jump right in!

Enjoy!

Carolyn

Table of Contents

Surfside

Make this fun and bright quilt with 20 fat quarters and a background fabric. It's easier than it looks.

Design by Gina Gempesaw
Quilted by Carole Whaling

Skill Level
Intermediate

Finished Size
Quilt Size: 58" x 70"
Block Size: 10" x 10" finished
Number of Blocks: 20

Materials
- 20 assorted fat quarters
- ⅝ yard coordinating stripe
- 2 yards white solid
- Backing to size
- Batting to size
- Thread
- Template material
- Basic sewing tools and supplies

Project Notes
Read all instructions before beginning this project. Stitch right sides together using a ¼" seam allowance unless otherwise specified. Refer to a favorite quilting guide for specific techniques. Materials and cutting lists assume 40" of usable fabric width.

Cutting
Prepare a template for the A triangle using pattern given. Mark the dot on the seam allowance at the tip on the template.

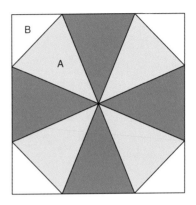

Surfside
10" x 10" Finished Block
Make 20

From each fat quarter:
- Cut 8 A triangles from each fat quarter (160 total) using the prepared template. Stack and pin in matching sets of 4 triangles.
- Cut a total of 68 (3" x 6½") G rectangles.

From coordinating stripe:
- Cut 7 (2¼" by fabric width) binding strips.

From white solid:
- Cut 4 (3¾" by fabric width) strips.
    Subcut strips into 40 (3¾") squares. Cut each
        square in half on 1 diagonal to make
        80 B triangles.
- Cut 1 (10½" by fabric width) strip.
    Subcut strip into 15 (1¾" x 10½") C strips.
- Cut 5 (1¾" by fabric width) D strips.
- Cut 3 (2⅝" by fabric width) E strips.
- Cut 3 (3" by fabric width) F strips.
- Cut 2 (3" by fabric width) strips.
    Subcut strips into 4 each 3" x 8½" J strips,
        3" x 6" H strips and 3" I squares.

Here's a Tip

Block pieces are cut on the bias. To help prevent stretching of pieces during piecing, apply spray starch or sizing to the wrong side of fabrics before cutting.

Completing the Blocks

1. To complete one Surfside block, select two different-color sets of four matching A triangles and four B triangles.

2. Join one A triangle from each fabric to make an A unit, stopping stitching at the inside point on the marked dot as shown in Figure 1; press. Repeat to make a total of four A units.

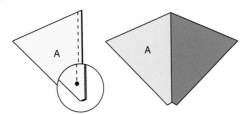

Figure 1

3. Join two A units to make half the block, again stopping at the marked point as shown in Figure 2; press. Repeat to make the second half of the block.

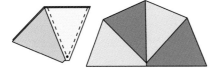

Figure 2

4. Join the two block halves, stopping stitching at the marked dots to complete the center section as shown in Figure 3.

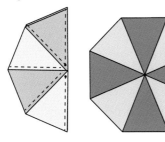

Figure 3

5. Press the center points to reduce bulk as shown in Figure 4 and in Spinning Centers to Reduce Bulk on page 8.

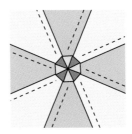 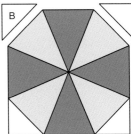

Figure 4   **Figure 5**

6. Sew a B triangle to each corner to complete one Surfside block as shown in Figure 5; press.

7. Repeat steps 1–6 to complete a total of 20 Surfside blocks.

Completing the Quilt Top

Refer to the Assembly Diagram for row piecing and arrangement as needed.

1. Arrange and join four Surfside blocks with three C strips to make a row; press. Repeat to make a total of five rows.

2. Join the D strips on the short ends to make a long strip; press. Subcut strip into four 1¾" x 44¼" D strips.

3. Join the pieced rows with the D strips to complete the quilt center; press.

4. Join the E strips on the short ends to make a long strip; press. Subcut strip into two 2⅝" x 55½" E strips. Sew these strips to opposite long sides of the quilt center; press.

5. Join the F strips on the short ends to make a long strip; press. Subcut strip into two 3" x 48½" F strips. Sew these strips to the top and bottom of the quilt center; press.

6. Select and join 10 G rectangles on the short ends to make a pieced side strip; press. Repeat to make a second pieced side strip. Sew these strips to opposite long sides of the quilt center; press.

Surfside
Assembly Diagram 58" x 70"

7. Select and join eight G rectangles with two I squares to make a pieced top strip; press. Repeat to make a pieced bottom strip. Sew these strips to the top and bottom of the quilt center; press.

8. Select and join nine G rectangles and add an H rectangle to each end to make a pieced side strip; press. Repeat to make a second pieced side strip. Sew these strips to opposite sides of the quilt center; press.

9. Select and join seven G rectangles and add a J strip to each end to make the pieced top strip; press. Repeat to make the pieced bottom strip. Sew these strips to the top and bottom of the quilt center to complete the quilt top.

Completing the Quilt

1. Sandwich the batting between the pieced top and a prepared backing piece; baste layers together. Quilt as desired.

2. When quilting is complete, remove basting and trim batting and backing fabric even with raw edges of the pieced top.

3. Prepare binding and stitch to quilt front edges, matching raw edges, mitering corners and overlapping ends. Fold binding to back side and stitch in place. ●

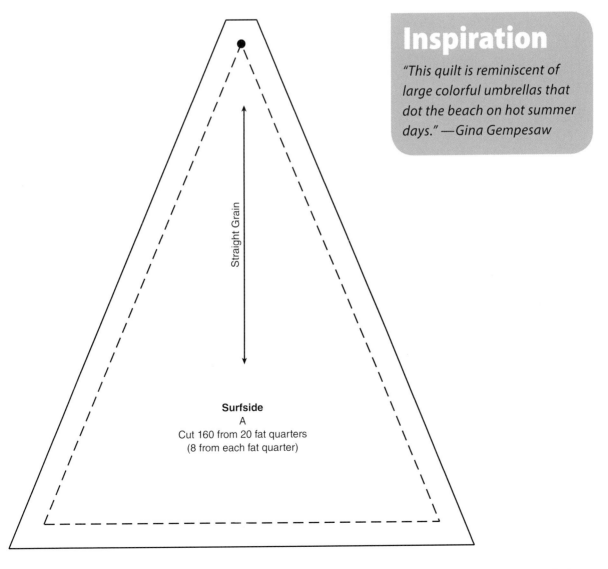

Straight Grain

Surfside
A
Cut 160 from 20 fat quarters
(8 from each fat quarter)

Inspiration

"This quilt is reminiscent of large colorful umbrellas that dot the beach on hot summer days." —Gina Gempesaw

Spinning Centers to Reduce Bulk

When sewing a block where numerous points meet together, there can be a lot of "bulk" in the seam allowance on the wrong side of the fabric. This extra bulk prohibits the block from lying flat when pressed. One option is to trim the points off thus reducing the amount of fabric in the seam allowance. Another option is to "spin" the center of the seam allowances thus distributing the bulk more evenly.

1. Stitch the block as usual, nesting seams at any intersection (Photo A).

Photo A

2. Before pressing, remove approximately three stitches in the seam allowance from each side of the previously sewn seams (Photo B).

Photo B

3. Place the block on a pressing board right side down (Photo C).

Photo C

4. With your finger, push the top seam to the right and the bottom seam to the left. This will result in the seam allowances spinning in a clockwise direction (Photo D).

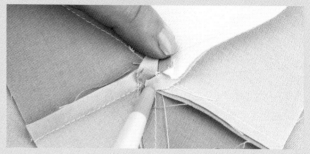

Photo D

5. The center will pop open and the seam allowances will swirl around the center of the block (Photo E).

Photo E

6. Press with an iron to flatten the seam allowances in place (Photo F).

Photo F

Splash!

The large blocks and unusual construction make this an easy and fun project.

Design by Lyn Brown
Quilted by Jami Goto

Skill Level

Confident Beginner

Finished Size

Quilt Size: 57" x 74"
Block Size: 15" x 15" finished
Number of Blocks: 12

Materials

- 1⅔ yards white batik
- 3⅞ yards blue batik
- Backing to size
- Batting to size
- Thread
- Mechanical pencil or fine-point permanent marker
- Basic sewing tools and supplies

Project Notes

Read all instructions before beginning this project. Stitch right sides together using a ¼" seam allowance unless otherwise specified. Refer to a favorite quilting guide for specific techniques. Materials and cutting lists assume 40" of usable fabric width.

Cutting

From white batik:

- Cut 6 (8⅜" by fabric width) A strips.

From blue batik:

- Cut 6 (8¾" by fabric width) strips.
  Subcut strips into 48 (4⅜" x 8¾") B/BR rectangles.

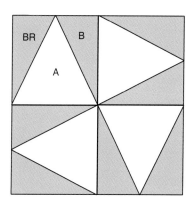

Splash
15" x 15" Finished Block
Make 12

- From the remaining length of fabric cut the following:
  2 (4½" x 57½") F strips
  2 (4½" x 66½") E strips
  2 (2½" x 66½") D strips
  4 (2¼" by length of fabric) binding strips
  9 (2½" x 15½") C strips

Completing the Blocks

1. Trim selvage edges off one A strip. Using a ruler and a mechanical pencil or fine-point permanent marker, measure in 4⅛" from one trimmed end and make a tiny tick mark as shown in Figure 1. Continue making tick marks every 8¼" along the strip. This is the bottom edge.

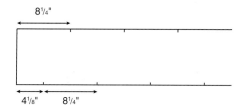

Figure 1

2. Make tick marks every 8¼" along the top of the strip, again referring to Figure 1. *Note: The top tick marks should be centered between two bottom tick marks.*

3. Position a straightedge at the top corner and align with the first bottom tick mark and cut as shown in Figure 2. Place the straightedge at the bottom tick mark and align with the next top tick mark and cut again to cut one A triangle. Continue across the width of the strip to cut seven more A triangles from the same strip.

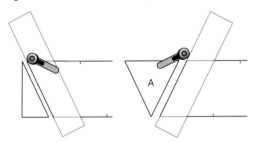

Figure 2

4. Repeat steps 1–3 with remaining A strips to cut 48 A triangles.

5. Place the B rectangles right side up in two equal piles of 24. Referring to Figure 3, cut the B rectangles in one pile from the upper left corner to the lower right corner to make 48 B triangles. Cut the second pile from the lower left corner to the upper right corner to make 48 BR triangles

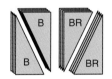

Figure 3

6. To complete one Splash block, select four each A, B and BR triangles.

7. Sew B and BR to A to make an A-B unit referring to Figure 4 and Triangle Alignment on page 13; press. Repeat to make four A-B units.

A-B Unit
Make 4

Figure 4

8. Join two A-B units to make a row as shown in Figure 5; press. Repeat to make a second row.

Make 2

Figure 5

9. Join the rows to complete one Splash block as shown in Figure 6; press.

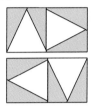

Figure 6

10. Repeat steps 6–9 to complete a total of 12 Splash blocks.

Completing the Quilt Top

Refer to the Assembly Diagram as needed.

1. Arrange and join three C strips with four Splash blocks to make one vertical row; press. Repeat to make a total of three vertical rows.

2. Join the vertical rows with two D strips to complete the quilt center; press.

3. Sew E strips to opposite long sides and F strips to the top and bottom of the quilt center to complete the quilt top; press.

Completing the Quilt

1. Sandwich the batting between the pieced top and a prepared backing piece; baste layers together. Quilt as desired.

2. When quilting is complete, remove basting and trim batting and backing fabric even with raw edges of the pieced top.

3. Prepare binding and stitch to quilt front edges, matching raw edges, mitering corners and overlapping ends. Fold binding to back side and stitch in place. ●

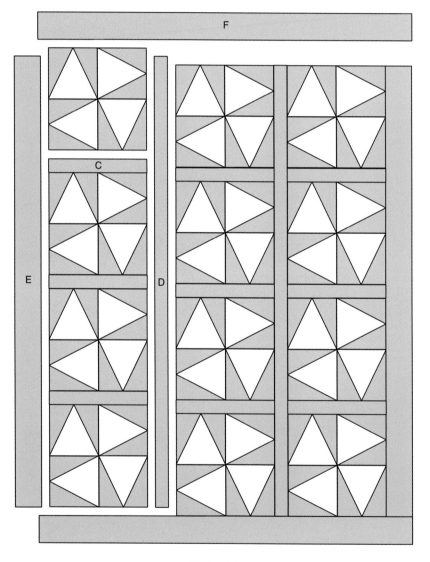

Splash!
Assembly Diagram 57" x 74"

Triangle Alignment

Position a B triangle right sides together on top of an A triangle, aligning long edges referring to Figure A.

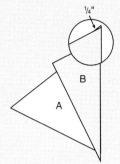

When you take the first stitch at the point of the A triangle, the needle should go through both pieces right at the ¼" seam allowance as shown in Figure B.

Figure A

Figure B

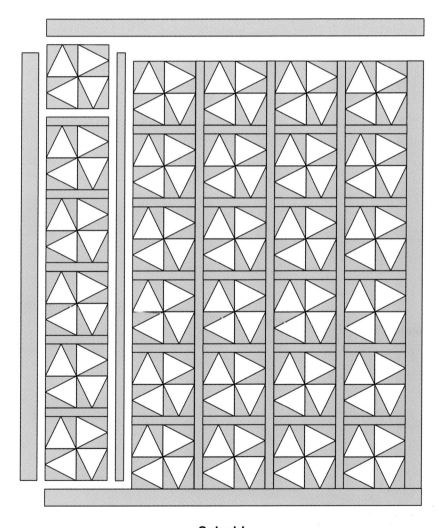

Splash!
Alternate Assembly Diagram 91" x 108"
Add 2 more rows and D strips to the width
and 2 more blocks and C strips to the length
to make a queen-size quilt.

Batik Jewels

Batik scraps appear to float through the solid background fabric leaving lots of open space for creative quilting.

Designed & Quilted by Holly Daniels

Skill Level
Confident Beginner

Finished Size
Quilt Size: 55" x 60"
Block Size: 7" x 6" finished
Number of Blocks: 32

Materials
- 32 (7" x 6½") rectangles assorted batiks
- 1 yard dark pink tonal
- 3⅓ yards white solid
- Backing to size
- Batting to size
- Thread
- Basic sewing tools and supplies

Project Notes
Read all instructions before beginning this project. Stitch right sides together using a ¼" seam allowance unless otherwise specified. Refer to a favorite quilting guide for specific techniques. Materials and cutting lists assume 40" of usable fabric width.

Cutting

From assorted batiks:
- Cut each 7" x 6½" rectangle in half to make 2 (3½" x 6½") A rectangles to total 64 A rectangles.

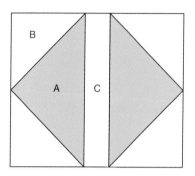

Batik Jewel
7" x 6" Finished Block
Make 32

From dark pink tonal:
- Cut 6 (1½" by fabric width) G/H strips.
- Cut 7 (2¼" by fabric width) binding strips.

From white solid:
- Cut 12 (3½" by fabric width) strips.
  Subcut strips into 128 (3½") B squares.
- Cut 8 (6½" by fabric width) strips.
  Subcut strips into 32 (1½" x 6½") C strips and 31 (7½" x 6½") D rectangles.
- Cut 6 (2½" by fabric width) E/F strips.

Completing the Blocks
1. Draw a line from corner to corner on the wrong side of each B square.

2. Select one A rectangle and two B squares. Referring to Figure 1, place a B square right sides together on one end of A and stitch on the marked line; trim seam to ¼" and press B to the right side.

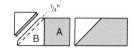

Figure 1

3. Repeat step 2 with a second B square on the opposite end of A to complete one A-B unit as shown in Figure 2; press.

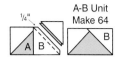

Figure 2

4. Repeat steps 2 and 3 with all A and B pieces to make a total of 64 A-B units (32 matching sets of two).

5. To complete one Jewel block, select two matching A-B units and a C strip.

6. Join the two A-B units with C to complete one Jewel block as shown in Figure 3; press.

Figure 3

7. Repeat steps 5 and 6 to complete a total of 32 Jewel blocks.

Batik Jewels
Assembly Diagram 55" x 60"

Completing the Quilt Top

Refer to the Assembly Diagram for row piecing and arrangement as needed.

1. Arrange and join three D rectangles and four Jewel blocks to make row 1; press. Repeat to make a total of five rows.

2. Repeat step 1 with three Jewel blocks and four D rectangles to make row 2; press. Repeat to make a total of four rows.

3. Join the rows to complete the quilt center; press.

4. Join the E/F strips on the short ends to make a long strip; press. Subcut strip into two each 2½" x 49½" E strips and 2½" x 58½" F strips.

5. Sew E strips to the top and bottom, and F strips to opposite long sides of the quilt center; press.

6. Repeat step 4 with G/H strips to cut two each 1½" x 53½" G strips and 1½" x 60½" H strips.

7. Sew G strips to the top and bottom, and H strips to opposite long sides of the quilt center to complete the quilt top; press.

Completing the Quilt

1. Sandwich the batting between the pieced top and a prepared backing piece; baste layers together. Quilt as desired.

2. When quilting is complete, remove basting and trim batting and backing fabric even with raw edges of the pieced top.

3. Prepare binding and stitch to quilt front edges, matching raw edges, mitering corners and overlapping ends. Fold binding to back side and stitch in place. ●

Spinning Triangles

The triangles seem to spin out from the center of this quilt, causing the eye to perceive lots of movement.

Designed & Quilted by Sharon Tucker of Grass Roots Quilt Studio

Skill Level
Confident Beginner

Finished Size
Quilt Size: 54" x 54"

Materials
- ⅓ yard each 4 gold/rust batiks
- ⅜ yard 1 additional gold/rust batik
- 3⅛ yards tan solid
- Backing to size
- Batting to size
- Thread
- Basic sewing tools and supplies

Project Notes
Read all instructions before beginning this project. Stitch right sides together using a ¼" seam allowance unless otherwise specified. Refer to a favorite quilting guide for specific techniques. Materials and cutting lists assume 40" of usable fabric width.

Cutting

From gold/rust batiks:
- Cut 1 (3⅞" by fabric width) strip each fabric. Subcut strip into 10 (3⅞") C squares (50 total).
- Cut 1 (2¼" by fabric width) strip from 4 fabrics and 2 (2¼" by fabric width) strips from the additional fabric for binding (6 strips total).

From tan solid:
- Cut 5 (3⅞" by fabric width) strips. Subcut strips into 50 (3⅞") B squares.
- Cut 3 (3½" by fabric width) strips. Subcut strips into 8 (3½") A squares and 4 (3½" x 12½") E strips.
- Cut 3 (6½" by fabric width) strips. Subcut strips into 28 (3½" x 6½") F strips.
- Cut 5 (9½" by fabric width) strips. Subcut strips into 48 (3½" x 9½") D strips.

Completing the Triangle Units

1. Draw a line from corner to corner on the wrong side of each B square.

2. Place one B square right sides together with one C square and stitch ¼" on each side of the marked line as shown in Figure 1.

Figure 1

3. Cut the stitched unit apart on the marked line, open and press to make two B-C units as shown in Figure 2.

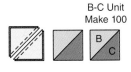

B-C Unit
Make 100

Figure 2

4. Repeat steps 2 and 3 with remaining B and C squares to make a total of 100 B-C units.

Completing the Quilt Top

1. Arrange and join the B-C units with the A squares and the D, E and F strips in 18 vertical rows referring to the Assembly Diagram for positioning of pieces in each row. **Note:** *Pay close attention to the orientation of the rows on each side of the center.*

2. Join the rows to complete the quilt top; press.

Inspiration

"Pinwheels at the beach provided the inspiration for this quilt. I thought of the triangles flying off the main pinwheel." —Sharon Tucker

Completing the Quilt

1. Sandwich the batting between the pieced top and a prepared backing piece; baste layers together. Quilt as desired.

2. When quilting is complete, remove basting and trim batting and backing fabric even with raw edges of the pieced top.

3. Prepare binding and stitch to quilt front edges, matching raw edges, mitering corners and overlapping ends. Fold binding to back side and stitch in place. ●

Spinning Triangles
Assembly Diagram 54" x 54"

Using Half-Square Triangle Piecing Papers

Streamline the piecing process and make perfect pieced half-square triangle units using triangle piecing paper. This paper is made to break away when not needed, and the ink is heatproof, so it will not smear ink on the fabrics.

The process is easy. Purchase the paper product—such as Thangles Half-Square Triangle Paper or Triangles on a Roll. Cut strips ½" wider than the finished size of triangle units; for example, for a 3" finished unit, cut 3½"-wide strips.

Layer the fabric strips right sides together and pin a paper pattern right side up on top of the strips. Sew on the marked dotted lines as shown in Figure A.

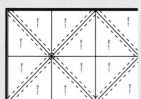

Figure A

Cut apart on the solid lines and trim off the dog ears on one end (Figure B).

Figure B

Press the two resulting units open with the paper still attached to support the bias seam.

Remove the paper; the half-square triangle units are the perfect size to be used in your project.

Tipsy Triangles

A classic pattern from the past updated with fresh vibrant solids is still in fashion.

Design by Nancy Scott
Quilted by Masterpiece Quilting

Skill Level
Advanced

Finished Size
Quilt Size: Approximately 62" x 62"
Block Sizes: 11" x 11" finished, 11" x 11" x 15½" finished
and 7¾" x 7¾" x 11" finished
Number of Blocks: 25, 12 and 4

Materials
- 3⅛ yards red solid
- 3⅔ yards white solid
- Backing to size
- Batting to size
- Thread
- Basic sewing tools and supplies

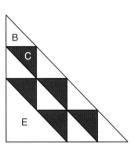

Corner Triangle
7¾" x 7¾" x 11" Finished Block
Make 2

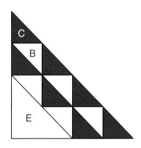

Reversed Corner Triangle
7¾" x 7¾" x 11" Finished Block
Make 2

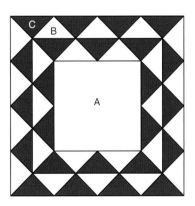

Tipsy Triangles
11" x 11" Finished Block
Make 25

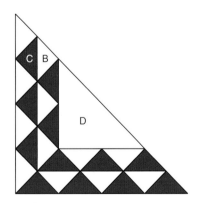

Side Triangle
11" x 11" x 15½" Finished Block
Make 6

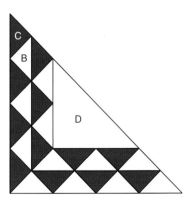

Reversed Side Triangle
11" x 11" x 15½" Finished Block
Make 6

Project Notes

Read all instructions before beginning this project. Stitch right sides together using a ¼" seam allowance unless otherwise specified. Refer to a favorite quilting guide for specific techniques. Materials and cutting lists assume 40" of usable fabric width.

Cutting

From red solid:
- Cut 20 (4" by fabric width) strips.
    Subcut strips into 192 (4") squares.
        Cut each square on both diagonals to make 768 C triangles.
- Cut 7 (2¼" by fabric width) binding strips.

From white solid:
- Cut 5 (6" by fabric width) strips.
    Subcut strips into 25 (6") A squares and 2 (4¾") E squares. Cut each E square in half on 1 diagonal to make 4 E triangles.
- Cut 20 (4" by fabric width) strips.
    Subcut strips into 192 (4") squares.
        Cut each square on both diagonals to make 768 B triangles.
- Cut 1 (9" by fabric width) strip.
    Subcut strip into 3 (9") squares. Cut each square on both diagonals to make 12 D triangles

Completing the Tipsy Triangles Blocks

1. Using a water-erasable marker or pencil, mark a small dot ¼" from edges at each corner of each A square as shown in Figure 1.

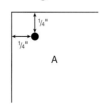

Figure 1

2. Join five B triangles with seven C triangles to make a B-C side unit as shown in Figure 2; press. Repeat to make a total of 64 B-C side units.

B-C Side Unit
Make 64

Figure 2

3. Join five C triangles with seven B triangles to make a C-B side unit as shown in Figure 3; press. Repeat to make a total of 64 C-B side units. **Note:** *Set aside 14 each B-C and C-B side units for Side Triangle and Corner Triangle blocks.*

C-B Side Unit
Make 64

Figure 3

4. To complete one Tipsy Triangles block, select one A square and two each B-C and C-B side units.

5. Locking stitches at the beginning and end of each seam, sew a B-C side unit to opposite sides of the A square, stopping stitching at the marked dots on A as shown in Figure 4.

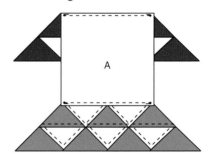

Figure 4

6. Repeat step 5 with the C-B side units on the remaining sides of A as shown in Figure 5.

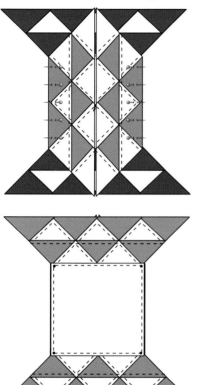

Figure 5

7. Starting at the outer edge of one corner, stitch to the marked dot on A as shown in Figure 6; secure seam and press. Repeat on each corner to complete one Tipsy Triangles block.

Figure 6

8. Repeat steps 4–7 to complete a total of 25 Tipsy Triangles blocks.

Completing the Side Triangle Blocks

1. Select one D triangle and one each B-C and C-B side unit to complete one Side Triangle block.

2. Sew the B-C side unit to the bottom edge and the C-B side unit to the left edge of D and stitch the corner seam referring to Completing the Tipsy Triangles Blocks to complete one Side Triangle block as shown in Figure 7; press.

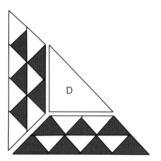

Figure 7

3. Repeat steps 1 and 2 to complete a total of six Side Triangle blocks.

4. Repeat steps 1 and 2 except sew the B-C side unit to the left edge and the C-B side unit to the bottom of D to complete six Reversed Side Triangle blocks referring to Figure 8.

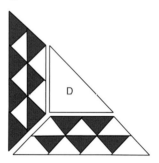

Figure 8

Completing the Corner Triangle Blocks

1. To complete one Corner Triangle block, select one E triangle and one C-B side unit.

2. Sew the C-B side unit to the long edge of E to complete one Corner Triangle block as shown in Figure 9; press. Repeat to make a second Corner Triangle block.

3. To complete one Reversed Corner Triangle block, select one each E triangle and B-C side unit.

4. Sew the B-C side unit to the long edge of E to complete one Reversed Corner Triangle block as shown in Figure 10; press. Repeat to make a second Reversed Corner Triangle block.

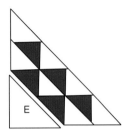

Figure 9

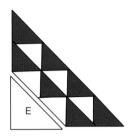

Figure 10

Completing the Quilt Top

Refer to the Assembly Diagram for row piecing and arrangement as needed.

1. Arrange and join the Tipsy Triangles blocks in diagonal rows with the Reversed Side and Side Triangle blocks and the Reversed Corner Triangle blocks; press.

2. Join the pieced diagonal rows and add the Corner Triangle blocks to complete the quilt top; press.

Completing the Quilt

1. Sandwich the batting between the pieced top and a prepared backing piece; baste layers together. Quilt as desired.

2. When quilting is complete, remove basting and trim batting and backing fabric even with raw edges of the pieced top.

3. Prepare binding and stitch to quilt front edges, matching raw edges, mitering corners and overlapping ends. Fold binding to back side and stitch in place. ●

Inspiration

"This quilt is a replica of an antique quilt I purchased at auction, made using the same construction techniques." —Nancy Scott

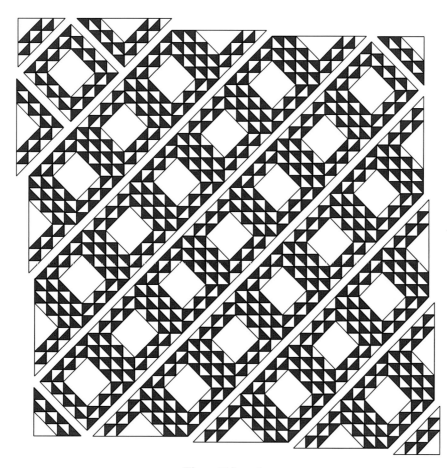

Tipsy Triangles
Assembly Diagram Approximately 62" x 62"

Woven Web

Careful color selection and placement, and a 60-degree equilateral triangle ruler are all you need to make this woven quilt. Imagine your color palette in this pattern.

Design by Nancy Scott
Quilted by Masterpiece Quilting

Skill Level
Confident Beginner

Finished Size
Quilt Size: 42" x 61"

Materials
- ⅞ yard yellow tonal
- 1½ yards black tonal
- 2 yards purple tonal
- Backing to size
- Batting to size
- Thread
- Template material or 60-degree triangle ruler
- Basic sewing tools and supplies

Project Notes
Read all instructions before beginning this project. Stitch right sides together using a ¼" seam allowance unless otherwise specified. Refer to a favorite quilting guide for specific techniques. Materials and cutting lists assume 40" of usable fabric width.

Cutting
Prepare a template for the A triangle using pattern given. See Using a 60-Degree Triangle Ruler on page 32 if using a purchased ruler to cut the A pieces and determine size to cut strips.

From yellow tonal:
- Cut 6 (4¼" by fabric width) strips.
  Subcut strips into 90 A triangles.

From black tonal:
- Cut 6 (4¼" by fabric width) strips.
  Subcut strips into 90 A triangles.
- Cut 6 (2¼" by fabric width) binding strips.

From purple tonal:
- Cut 13 (4¼" by fabric width) strips.
  Subcut strips into 192 A triangles.

Completing the Quilt Top
Refer to the Assembly Diagram to arrange rows as needed.

1. Arrange and join seven black, eight yellow and 16 purple A triangles to make an A row referring to Figure 1; press. Repeat to make a total of six A rows.

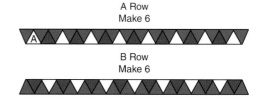

A Row
Make 6

B Row
Make 6

Figure 1

2. Arrange and join seven yellow, eight black and 16 purple A triangles to make a B row, again referring to Figure 1. Repeat to make a total of six B rows.

3. Sew an A row to a B row to make a row section as shown in Figure 2; press. Repeat to make six row sections.

Row Section
Make 6

Figure 2

4. Join the row sections, rotating the sections to form the pattern to complete the pieced top; press.

5. Using a rotary cutter and ruler, trim the purple A triangles at the top and bottom of the quilt, leaving ¼" beyond yellow and black triangle corners to square the quilt center referring to Figure 3.

¼"

Figure 3

Woven Web
Assembly Diagram 42" x 61"

Using a 60-Degree Triangle Ruler

If you like to rotary-cut all of your pieces, purchased tools are available to eliminate making your own templates. The tools are thicker and allow for cutting the required-size strips and then using a rotary cutter to cut the individual pieces. Several different brands of 60-degree rulers could be used to make this quick quilt.

Rulers are available in two styles. One style has the tips blunted off. If you have this style, cut the strips 4" wide and then use the template to cut the pieces as shown in Figure A.

4"

Figure A

If you have a 60-degree triangle ruler with pointed tips, the 4¼"-wide strip given in the instructions will work perfectly.

Completing the Quilt

1. Sandwich the batting between the pieced top and a prepared backing piece; baste layers together. Quilt as desired.

2. When quilting is complete, remove basting and trim batting and backing fabric even with raw edges of the pieced top.

3. Prepare binding and stitch to quilt front edges, matching raw edges, mitering corners and overlapping ends. Fold binding to back side and stitch in place. ●

Inspiration

"This quilt design came about purely by accident. I was playing with hexagons in my design software and ended up with a woven web!" —Nancy Scott

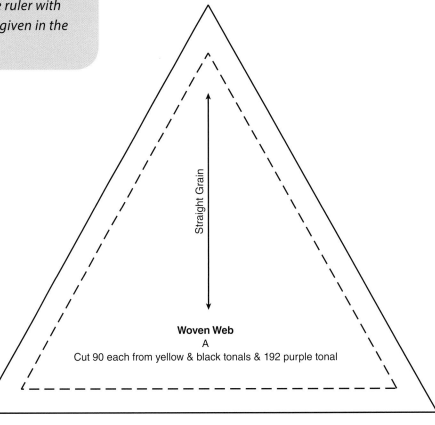

Straight Grain

Woven Web
A
Cut 90 each from yellow & black tonals & 192 purple tonal

Woven Web
Alternate Assembly Diagram 63" x 93½"
Add 3 each A and B vertical rows
to the width and 16 triangles
to the length to make a twin-size quilt.

Garden Walk

Using the same quilt block in different sizes in the same quilt top can add visual interest to an otherwise simple design.

Designed & Quilted by Tricia Lynn Maloney

Skill Level
Confident Beginner

Finished Size
Quilt Size: 68" x 76"
Block Size: 9" x 9" finished
Number of Blocks: 36

Materials
- ⅞ yard green floral
- 1⅜ yards green-with-white dots
- 1½ yards brown large floral
- 2⅛ yards cream solid
- 2¼ yards peach floral
- Backing to size
- Batting to size
- Thread
- Basic sewing tools and supplies

Project Notes
Read all instructions before beginning this project. Stitch right sides together using a ¼" seam allowance unless otherwise specified. Refer to a favorite quilting guide for specific techniques. Materials and cutting lists assume 40" of usable fabric width.

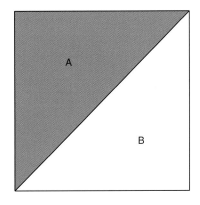

Peach Triangle
9" x 9" Finished Block
Make 4

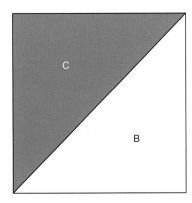

Green Triangle
9" x 9" Finished Block
Make 16

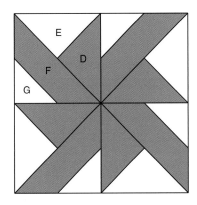

Garden Walk Quad
9" x 9" Finished Block
Make 12

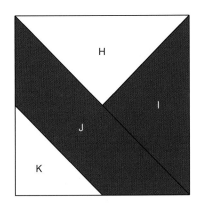

Garden Walk
9" x 9" Finished Block
Make 4

Cutting

From green floral:
- Cut 7 (3" by fabric width) M/N strips.
- Cut 1 (5" by fabric width) strip.
  Subcut strip into 4 (5") Q squares.

From green-with-white dots:
- Cut 2 (9⅞" by fabric width) strips.
  Subcut strips into 8 (9⅞") C squares.
- Cut 8 (2¼" by fabric width) binding strips.

From brown large floral:
- Cut 1 (10¼" by fabric width) strip.
  Subcut strip into 1 (10¼") I square and 2 (9⅞")
  J squares. Cut the I square on both diagonals
  to make 4 I triangles.
- Cut 7 (5" by fabric width) O/P strips.

From cream solid:
- Cut 3 (9⅞" by fabric width) strips.
  Subcut strips into 10 (9⅞") B squares.
- Cut 1 (10¼" by fabric width) strip.
  Subcut strip into 1 (10¼") H square and 4 (5")
  K squares. Cut the H square on both diagonals
  to make 4 H triangles.
- Cut 2 (5¾" by fabric width) strips.
  Subcut strips into 12 (5¾") squares.
  Cut each square on both diagonals to
  make 48 E triangles.
- Cut 4 (2¾" by fabric width) strips.
  Subcut strips into 48 (2¾") G squares.

From peach floral:
- Cut 2 (5¾" by fabric width) strips.
  Subcut strips into 12 (5¾") squares.
  Cut each square on both diagonals to
  make 48 D triangles.
- Cut 4 (5⅜" by fabric width) strips.
  Subcut strips into 24 (5⅜") F squares.
- Cut 2 (9⅞" by fabric width) strips.
  Subcut strips into 2 (9⅞") A squares.
- Cut 3 (5" by fabric width) L strips.

Completing the Triangle Blocks

1. Draw a line from corner to corner on the wrong side of each B square.

2. Place a B square right sides together with an A square and stitch ¼" on each side of the marked line. Cut apart on the marked line and press units open to complete two Peach Triangle blocks as shown in Figure 1. Repeat to make a total of four Peach Triangle blocks.

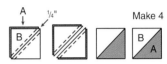

Figure 1

3. Repeat step 2 with B and C squares to make 16 Green Triangle blocks as shown in Figure 2.

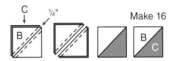

Figure 2

Completing the Garden Walk Quad Blocks

1. Draw a line from corner to corner on the wrong side of each G square.

2. Referring to Figure 3, place a G square right sides together on opposite corners of an F square and stitch on the marked lines. Trim the seam allowance to ¼" and press G to the right side. Cut in half on the unpieced diagonal of F to complete two F-G units. Repeat with remaining F and G pieces to make a total of 48 F-G units.

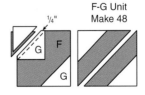

Figure 3

3. To complete one Garden Walk Quad block, select four each D and E triangles, and F-G units.

4. Sew D to E to make a D-E unit as shown in Figure 4; press. Repeat to make a total of four D-E units.

D-E Unit
Make 4

Figure 4

5. Sew a D-E unit to an F-G unit to make a block quarter as shown in Figure 5; press. Repeat to make a total of four block quarters.

Make 4

Figure 5

6. Join two block quarters to make a row as shown in Figure 6; press. Repeat to make a second row.

Make 2

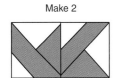

Figure 6

7. Join the rows to complete one Garden Walk Quad block referring to Figure 7; press.

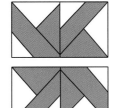

Figure 7

8. Repeat steps 3–7 to complete a total of 12 Garden Walk Quad blocks.

Completing the Garden Walk Blocks

1. Repeat steps 1 and 2 of Completing the Garden Walk Quad Blocks to make four J-K units as shown in Figure 8.

J-K Unit
Make 4

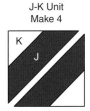

Figure 8

2. To complete one Garden Walk block, select one each H and I triangle, and one J-K unit.

3. Sew H to I to make an H-I unit as shown in Figure 9; press.

H-I Unit

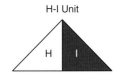

Figure 9

4. Sew the H-I unit to the J-K unit to complete one Garden Walk block as shown in Figure 10; press.

Figure 10

5. Repeat steps 2–4 to complete a total of four Garden Walk blocks.

Completing the Quilt Top

Refer to the Assembly Diagram for row piecing and arrangement as needed.

1. Arrange and join six blocks to make a row; press. Repeat to make a total of six rows.

2. Join the rows to complete the quilt center; press.

3. Join the L strips on the short ends to make a long strip; press. Subcut the strip into two 4" x 54½" L strips. Sew an L strip to the top and bottom of the quilt center; press.

4. Join the M/N strips on the short ends to make a long strip; press. Subcut the strip into two each 3" x 62½" M strips and 3" x 59½" N strips.

5. Sew the M strips to opposite long sides and N strips to the top and bottom of the quilt center; press.

6. Join the O/P strips on the short ends to make a long strip; press. Subcut strip into two each 5" x 67½" O strips and 5" x 59½" P strips.

7. Sew O strips to opposite sides of the quilt center; press. Sew a Q square to each end of each P strip; press. Sew the P-Q strips to the top and bottom of the quilt center to complete the quilt top; press.

Completing the Quilt

1. Sandwich the batting between the pieced top and a prepared backing piece; baste layers together. Quilt as desired.

2. When quilting is complete, remove basting and trim batting and backing fabric even with raw edges of the pieced top.

3. Prepare binding and stitch to quilt front edges, matching raw edges, mitering corners and overlapping ends. Fold binding to back side and stitch in place. ●

Garden Walk
Assembly Diagram 68" x 76"

Triangles 5.0

Just one block twisted and turned will create this stunning quilt.

Designed & Quilted by Bev Getschel

Skill Level
Confident Beginner

Finished Size
Quilt Size: 72" x 72"
Block Size: 6" x 6" finished
Number of Blocks: 144

Materials
- 1 yard cream batik
- 3¼ yards gray print batik
- 3⅓ yards black solid
- Backing to size
- Batting to size
- Thread
- Basic sewing tools and supplies

Project Notes
Read all instructions before beginning this project. Stitch right sides together using a ¼" seam allowance unless otherwise specified. Refer to a favorite quilting guide for specific techniques. Materials and cutting lists assume 40" of usable fabric width.

Cutting

From cream batik:
- Cut 8 (3⅞" by fabric width) strips.
   Subcut strips into 72 (3⅞") B squares.

From gray print batik:
- Cut 15 (6⅞" by fabric width) strips.
   Subcut strips into 72 (6⅞") squares.
      Cut each square in half on 1 diagonal to make 144 A triangles.

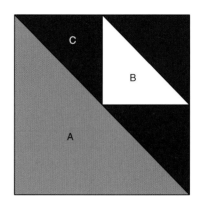

Triangles
6" x 6" Finished Block
Make 144

From black solid:
- Cut 22 (3⅞" by fabric width) strips.
   Subcut strips into 216 (3⅞") squares.
      Cut 144 squares in half on 1 diagonal to make 288 C triangles. Set aside remaining squares for B-C units.
- Cut 8 (2¼" by fabric width) binding strips.

Completing the Blocks
1. Mark a line from corner to corner on the wrong side of each B square.

2. Referring to Figure 1, place a marked B square right sides together with a C square and stitch ¼" on each side of the marked line. Cut apart on the marked line and press open to complete two B-C units.

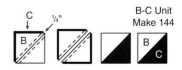

Figure 1

3. Repeat step 2 to make a total of 144 B-C units.

4. To complete one Triangles block, select one A triangle, one B-C unit and two C triangles.

5. Sew a C triangle to the B sides of the B-C unit to complete a pieced triangle unit as shown in Figure 2; press.

Figure 2

6. Sew the A triangle to the long edge of the pieced triangle unit to complete one Triangles block as shown in Figure 3; press.

Figure 3

7. Repeat steps 4–6 to complete a total of 144 Triangles blocks.

Completing the Quilt Top

Refer to the Assembly Diagram for positioning of blocks in rows to form the pattern.

1. Arrange and join 12 Triangles blocks to make a block row; press. Repeat to make a total of 12 rows.

2. Join the rows to complete the quilt top; press.

Completing the Quilt

1. Sandwich the batting between the pieced top and a prepared backing piece; baste layers together. Quilt as desired.

2. When quilting is complete, remove basting and trim batting and backing fabric even with raw edges of the pieced top.

3. Prepare binding and stitch to quilt front edges, matching raw edges, mitering corners and overlapping ends. Fold binding to back side and stitch in place. ●

Inspiration

"Both of my sons-in-law are named David. Our grandson Michael referred to them as David 2.0. It clicked with me, 'this is the name'—the block has five triangles, thus Triangles 5.0!"
—Bev Getschel

Triangles 5.0
Assembly Diagram 72" x 72"

Quilting Basics

The following is a reference guide. For more information, consult a comprehensive quilting book.

Always:

- Read through the entire pattern before you begin your project.
- Purchase quality, 100 percent cotton fabrics.
- When considering prewashing, do so with ALL of the fabrics being used. Generally, prewashing is not required in quilting.
- Use ¼" seam allowance for all stitching unless otherwise instructed.
- Use a short-to-medium stitch length.
- Make sure your seams are accurate.

Quilting Tools & Supplies

- Rotary cutter and mat
- Scissors for paper and fabric
- Non-slip quilting rulers
- Marking tools
- Sewing machine
- Sewing machine feet:
    ¼" seaming foot (for piecing)
    Walking or even-feed foot (for piecing or quilting)
    Darning or free-motion foot (for free-motion quilting)
- Quilting hand-sewing needles
- Straight pins
- Curved safety pins for basting
- Seam ripper
- Iron and ironing surface

Basic Techniques

Appliqué

Fusible Appliqué

All templates in *Quilter's World* are reversed for use with this technique.

1. Trace the instructed number of templates ¼" apart onto the paper side of paper-backed fusible web. Cut apart the templates, leaving a margin around each, and fuse to the wrong side of the fabric following fusible web manufacturer's instructions.

2. Cut the appliqué pieces out on the traced lines, remove paper backing and fuse to the background referring to the appliqué motif given.

3. Finish appliqué raw edges with a straight, satin, blanket, zigzag or blind-hem machine stitch with matching or invisible thread.

Turned-Edge Appliqué

1. Trace the printed reversed templates onto template plastic. Flip the template over and mark as the right side.

2. Position the template, right side up, on the right side of fabric and lightly trace, spacing images ½" apart. Cut apart, leaving a ¼" margin around the traced lines.

3. Clip curves and press edges ¼" to the wrong side around the appliqué shape.

4. Referring to the appliqué motif, pin or baste appliqué shapes to the background.

5. Hand-stitch shapes in place using a blind stitch and thread to match or machine-stitch using a short blind hemstitch and either matching or invisible thread.

Borders

Most *Quilter's World* patterns give an exact size to cut borders. You may check those sizes by comparing them to the horizontal and vertical center measurements of your quilt top.

Straight Borders

1. Mark the centers of the side borders and quilt top sides.

2. Stitch borders to quilt top sides with right sides together and matching raw edges and center marks using a ¼" seam. Press seams toward borders.

3. Repeat with top and bottom border lengths.

Mitered Borders

1. Add at least twice the border width to the border lengths instructed to cut.

2. Center and sew the side borders to the quilt, beginning and ending stitching ¼" from the quilt corner and backstitching (Figure 1). Repeat with the top and bottom borders.

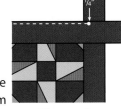

Figure 1

3. Fold and pin quilt right sides together at a 45-degree angle on one corner (Figure 2). Place a straightedge along the fold and lightly mark a line across the border ends.

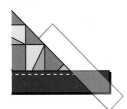

Figure 2

4. Stitch along the line, backstitching to secure. Trim seam to ¼" and press open (Figure 3).

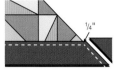

Figure 3

Quilt Backing & Batting

We suggest that you cut your backing and batting 8" larger than the finished quilt-top size. If preparing the backing from standard-width fabrics, remove the selvages and sew two or three lengths together; press seams open. If using 108"-wide fabric, trim to size on the straight grain of the fabric.

Prepare batting the same size as your backing. You can purchase prepackaged sizes or battings by the yard and trim to size.

Quilting

1. Press quilt top on both sides and trim all loose threads.

2. Make a quilt sandwich by layering the backing right side down, batting and quilt top centered right side up on flat surface and smooth out. Pin or baste layers together to hold.

3. Mark quilting design on quilt top and quilt as desired by hand or machine. *Note: If you are sending your quilt to a professional quilter, contact them for specifics about preparing your quilt for quilting.*

4. When quilting is complete, remove pins or basting. Trim batting and backing edges even with raw edges of quilt top.

Binding the Quilt

1. Join binding strips on short ends with diagonal seams to make one long strip; trim seams to ¼" and press seams open (Figure 4).

2. Fold 1" of one short end to wrong side and press. Fold the binding strip in half with wrong sides together along length, again referring to Figure 4; press.

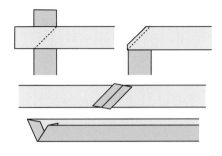

Figure 4

3. Starting about 3" from the folded short end, sew binding to quilt top edges, matching raw edges and using a ¼" seam. Stop stitching ¼" from corner and backstitch (Figure 5).

Figure 5

4. Fold binding up at a 45-degree angle to seam and then down even with quilt edges, forming a pleat at corner, referring to Figure 6.

Figure 6

5. Resume stitching from corner edge as shown in Figure 6, down quilt side, backstitching ¼" from next corner. Repeat, mitering all corners, stitching to within 3" of starting point.

6. Trim binding end long enough to tuck inside starting end and complete stitching (Figure 7).

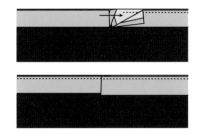

Figure 7

7. Fold binding to quilt back and stitch in place by hand or machine to complete your quilt.

Quilting Terms

- **Appliqué:** Adding fabric motifs to a foundation fabric by hand or machine (see Appliqué section of Basic Techniques).

- **Basting:** This temporarily secures layers of quilting materials together with safety pins, thread or a spray adhesive in preparation for quilting the layers.

  Use a long, straight stitch to hand- or machine-stitch one element to another holding the elements in place during construction and usually removed after construction.

- **Batting:** An insulating material made in a variety of fiber contents that is used between the quilt top and back to provide extra warmth and loft.

- **Binding:** A finishing strip of fabric sewn to the outer raw edges of a quilt to cover them.

  Straight-grain binding strips, cut on the crosswise straight grain of the fabric (see Straight & Bias Grain Lines illustration on page 62), are commonly used.

  Bias binding strips are cut at a 45-degree angle to the straight grain of the fabric. They are used when binding is being added to curved edges.

- **Block:** The basic quilting unit that is repeated to complete the quilt's design composition. Blocks can be pieced, appliquéd or solid and are usually square or rectangular in shape.
- **Border:** The frame of a quilt's central design used to visually complete the design and give the eye a place to rest.
- **Fabric Grain:** The fibers that run either parallel (lengthwise grain) or perpendicular (crosswise grain) to the fabric selvage are straight grain.

  Bias is any diagonal line between the lengthwise or crosswise grain. At these angles the fabric is less stable and stretches easily. The true bias of a woven fabric is a 45-degree angle between the lengthwise and crosswise grain lines.

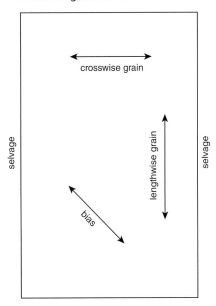

Straight & Bias Grain Lines

- **Mitered Corners:** Matching borders or turning bindings at a 45-degree angle at corners.
- **Patchwork:** A general term for the completed blocks or quilts that are made from smaller shapes sewn together.

- **Pattern:** This may refer to the design of a fabric or to the written instructions for a particular quilt design.
- **Piecing:** The act of sewing smaller pieces and/or units of a block or quilt together.

  Paper or foundation piecing is sewing fabric to a paper or cloth foundation in a certain order.

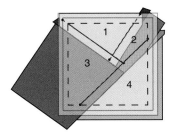

Foundation Piecing

String or chain piecing is sewing pieces together in a continuous string without clipping threads between sections.

String or Chain Piecing

- **Pressing:** Pressing is the process of placing the iron on the fabric, lifting it off the fabric and placing it down in another location to flatten seams or crease fabric without sliding the iron across the fabric.

  Quilters do not usually use steam when pressing, since it can easily distort fabric shapes.

  Generally, seam allowances are pressed toward the darker fabric in quilting so that they do not show through the lighter fabric.

  Seams are pressed in opposite directions where seams are being joined to allow seams to butt against each other and to distribute bulk.

Seams are pressed open when multiple seams come together in one place.

If you have a question about pressing direction, consult a comprehensive quilting guide for guidance.

- **Quilt (noun):** A sandwich of two layers of fabric with a third insulating material between them that is then stitched together with the edges covered or bound.
- **Quilt (verb):** Stitching several layers of fabric materials together with a decorative design. Stippling, cross-hatch, channel, in-the-ditch, free-motion, allover and meandering are all terms for quilting designs.

 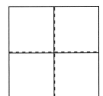

Meandering   **Stitch-in-the-ditch**

 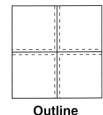

Channel   **Outline**

- **Quilt Sandwich:** A layer of insulating material between a quilt's top and back fabric.
- **Rotary Cutting:** Using a rotary cutting blade and straightedge to cut fabric.
- **Sashing:** Strips of fabric sewn between blocks to separate or set off the designs.
- **Subcut:** A second cutting of rotary-cut strips that makes the basic shapes used in block and quilt construction.
- **Template:** A pattern made from a sturdy material which is then used to cut shapes for patchwork and appliqué quilting.

Quilting Skill Levels

- **Beginner:** A quilter who has been introduced to the basics of cutting, piecing and assembling a quilt top and is working to master these skills. Someone who has the knowledge of how to sandwich, quilt and bind a quilt, but may not have necessarily accomplished the task yet.

- **Confident Beginner:** A quilter who has pieced and assembled several quilt tops and is comfortable with the process, and is now ready to move on to more challenging techniques and projects using at least two different techniques.

- **Intermediate:** A quilter who is comfortable with most quilting techniques and has a good understanding for design, color and the whole process. A quilter who is experienced in paper piecing, bias piecing and projects involving multiple techniques. Someone who is confident in making fabric selections other than those listed in the pattern.

- **Advanced:** A quilter who is looking for a challenging design. Someone who knows she or he can make any type of quilt. Someone who has the skills to read, comprehend and complete a pattern, and is willing to take on any technique. A quilter who is comfortable in her or his skills and has the ability to select fabric suited to the project. ●

Special Thanks

Please join us in thanking the talented designers
whose work is featured in this collection.

Lyn Brown
Splash!, page 9

Holly Daniels
Batik Jewels, page 15

Gina Gempesaw
Surfside, page 3

Bev Getschel
Triangles 5.0, page 40

Tricia Lynn Maloney
Garden Walk, page 34

Nancy Scott
Tipsy Triangles, page 22
Woven Web, page 29

Sharon Tucker
Spinning Triangles, page 18

Supplies

We would like to thank the following manufacturers who provided
materials to our designers to make sample projects for this book.

Batik Jewels, page 15: Warm & White® batting from The Warm Company.

Garden Walk, page 34: Roots & Wings fabric collection by Deena Rutter from Riley Blake; Quilter's 80/20 batting from Fairfield.

Spinning Triangles, page 18: Thangles Half-Square Triangle Paper.

Splash!, page 9: Batiks from Hoffman California Fabrics.

Surfside, page 3: Lola Textures fabric collection from Quilting Treasures.

Tipsy Triangles, page 22: AMB cotton solids from Clothworks; digital quilting patterns from TK Quilting & Design.

Triangles 5.0, page 40: Batiks from Hoffman California Fabrics; American Spirit 70/30 batting from Fairfield.

Woven Web, page 29: Floral Elements fabric collection by Pat Bravo for Art Gallery Fabrics; cotton batting from Bosal; digital quilting patterns from TK Quilting & Design.

Trendy Triangles is published by Annie's, 306 East Parr Road, Berne, IN 46711. Printed in USA. Copyright © 2015 Annie's. All rights reserved. This publication may not be reproduced in part or in whole without written permission from the publisher.

RETAIL STORES: If you would like to carry this publication or any other Annie's publications, visit AnniesWSL.com.

Every effort has been made to ensure that the instructions in this publication are complete and accurate. We cannot, however, take responsibility for human error, typographical mistakes or variations in individual work. Please visit AnniesCustomerService.com to check for pattern updates.

ISBN: 978-1-57367-954-1

1 2 3 4 5 6 7 8 9